Contents

Introduction

Pyrography is an ancient craft that has been practised worldwide for thousands of years. It involves the burning of designs on items, usually wooden, but it can also be used on leather, cork, fabric and paper. Traditionally, pyrography was used to decorate domestic utensils such as bowls, spoons and drinking vessels, but it has also been us... pieces of furniture, too. In this booklet are 18 simple step-by-step projects ... absolute beginner that provide the perfect introduction to this ancient and r... With a little practice you can personalize anything from spoons and keyrings... ambitious items such as bread boards. We're sure you'll enjoy this decorativ...

D1428695

Spoon

Wooden spoons are inexpensive to buy, make lovely gifts or bazaar items, and are an ideal project for the beginner.

MATERIALS
- Wooden spoon
- Pencil
- Rolled towel
- Drawing tip
- Eraser

TIP

Choose a spoon with a wide, flat rim when working a patterned edge.

1 Draw the design on the spoon freehand, using a towel to support it. Use the eraser to rub out any mistakes.

2 Still using the towel for support, begin to burn the outline of the design using the drawing tip.

3 Complete the outline using a simple line.

4 Start to add the fine detail to the design.

5 Complete the effect by adding lines that radiate from the outline. Use the eraser to rub out any pencil lines visible after the burning process.

The finished spoon

The drawing used

Coat Hanger

Pyrography is a great way to turn a basic household item into something that is beautiful as well as useful.

MATERIALS

- Plain wooden coat hanger
- Design to fit the front of the coat hanger
- Carbon paper
- Masking tape
- Ballpoint pen
- Drawing tip

TIP

Use a nursery motif and add a child's name to a hanger to encourage tidiness.

The drawing used

The finished coat hanger

1 Layer the carbon paper and the design and fix to the front of the coat hanger using masking tape.

2 Trace over the design firmly using a ballpoint pen.

3 Peel the carbon back carefully, making sure the design has transferred.

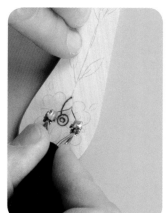

4 Burn the design onto the hanger using the drawing tip.

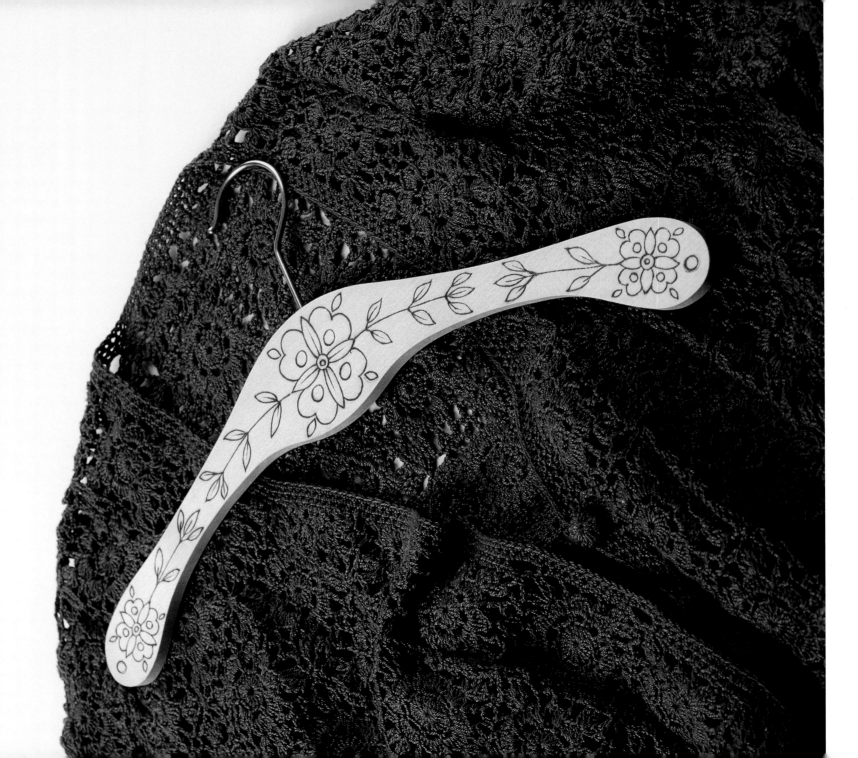

Jewelry Box

This pretty box is just right for keeping small trinkets safely, and can be worked to match any colour scheme.

MATERIALS

- Plain wooden box
- Design to fit lid
- Carbon paper
- Masking tape
- Ballpoint pen
- Rolled towel
- Drawing tip
- Felt-tipped pens

TIP

Line the box with felt and add a message to the inside of the lid.

1 Fix the carbon and the design to the top of the box using masking tape.

2 Using a towel to support your wrist, trace over the design firmly using a ballpoint pen.

3 Peel back the design, making sure it has transferred properly.

4 Begin to burn the outlines of the design using the drawing tip.

The finished box

5 Colour in the design, if desired, using felt-tipped pens.

The drawing used

Door Number

This number can be filled in simply or using a variety of patterns.
Filling in the background rather than the number gives a different look.

MATERIALS
- Wood blank
- Template
- Pencil
- Drawing tip
- Spoon point

TIP
The number can also be cut out using a small saw (see below).

1 Draw round the template carefully using a pencil.

2 Remove the template to reveal the outline of the number.

3 Burn the outline of the number using the drawing tip.

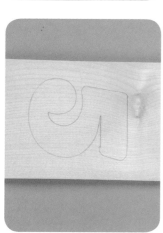

4 Stipple in the background of the number using an inverted spoon point.

5 Complete the background, keeping the tone as even as possible.

The blank used

Keyring

This little moon keyring is fun and quick to make, and can be personalized to suit people of all ages.

1 Draw round the template using a pencil.

2 Remove the template to reveal the outline of the design.

The completed design

3 Begin to burn the outline using the drawing tip.

4 Add a dot to represent an eye and burn the shape of the mouth.

5 Shade in the background with cross-hatching to finish.

MATERIALS
- Keyring blank
- Template
- Pencil
- Drawing tip

TIP
Make keyrings with different designs to suit the interests of the recipient.

The template used

Pencil Box

The design used for this box is based on a favourite stencil, but a completely freehand design would be equally suitable.

MATERIALS

- Pencil box blank
- Template
- Sharp pencil
- Drawing tip
- Eraser
- Felt-tipped pens (optional)

TIP

Make sure you leave enough space in the design to add a name.

The templates used

1 Place the butterfly template on the box and draw round it using a sharp pencil.

2 Draw the rest of the design freehand.

3 Burn the outlines using a drawing tip. Use the eraser to rub out any pencil lines visible after the burning process.

4 Colour in the design if desired, using felt-tipped pens.

The completed design, before the addition of colour

Coaster

Coasters are always useful, and you can make a matching set with just one pattern or a set that uses lots of different ones.

MATERIALS

- Plain wooden coaster
- Rubber stamp
- Ink pad
- Drawing tip

TIP

Do not overload the rubber stamp with ink. Stamp the first print on to scrap paper, as excess ink on the wood can cause bleeding.

1 Press the stamp firmly on the pad to ink it, then press on the centre of the blank.

2 Lift off the stamp to reveal the design in the centre of the coaster.

3 Burn the outline of the design using the drawing tip.

4 Still using the drawing tip, use stippling and stroking techniques to fill in the dark areas on the coaster.

5 Cross-hatch the background.

The rubber stamp used

The finished coaster

Letter Rack

This quickly worked item is a great way to tidy up those piles of letters that seem to accumulate all over the house.

MATERIALS
- Plain wooden letter rack
- Design to fit the front of the rack
- Carbon paper
- Masking tape
- Rolled towel
- Ballpoint pen
- Drawing tip

TIP
You could use someone's name or the word 'letters' as the main design on this.

The drawing used

1 Layer the carbon paper and the design and fix to the blank using masking tape.

2 Using the towel to support your wrist, trace over the design firmly with a ballpoint pen.

3 Peel the carbon back carefully, making sure the design has transferred completely.

4 Burn the outline of the design using the drawing tip.

5 Complete the shading.

The finished letter rack

Notepad

This is a great way to make sure you always have paper handy. Pads are easily replaced and attached using double-sided adhesive pads.

1 Layer the carbon paper and the design and fix to the blank using masking tape.

2 Trace over the design using a ballpoint pen and press firmly.

3 Peel the carbon back carefully, making sure all the design has transferred.

4 Burn the outline of the design using the drawing tip.

5 Complete the shading.

6 Attach the notepad using double-sided adhesive pads.

MATERIALS
- Wood blank
- Design to fit the front of the blank
- Carbon paper
- Masking tape
- Ballpoint pen
- Drawing tip
- Notepad
- Double-sided adhesive pads

TIP
Keep a pad by the telephone for messages and another in the kitchen for shopping lists.

The drawing used

The completed design

Mirror Frame

A floral pattern works very well with a mirror frame. Use felt-tipped pens to add colour if you wish.

MATERIALS
- Plain wooden mirror
- Design to fit edge of mirror
- Carbon paper
- Masking tape
- Ballpoint pen
- Drawing tip

TIP
If you want to make a mirror for a child, replace the mirror with mirrored perspex.

1 Fix the carbon and design to the mirror using masking tape.

2 Trace over the design firmly using a ballpoint pen.

3 Peel back the design carefully, making sure it has transferred correctly.

4 Burn the outline of the design.

5 Add the shading to the design.

The drawing used

The completed design

Butterfly Bowl

The design on this bowl is a popular motif, and it can be coloured using felt-tipped pens for a brighter effect.

MATERIALS
- Small turned bowl
- Butterfly template to fit rim
- Pencil
- Rolled towel
- Drawing tip
- Eraser

TIP
Use a ruler and a compass to mark out regularly spaced lines or draw freehand for a softer effect.

1 Pencil in the radiating lines first, then place the template on the edge of the bowl and draw round it with a pencil.

2 Using the towel to support your wrist, burn the radiating lines with a drawing tip.

3 Still using the drawing tip, burn the outline of the butterfly.

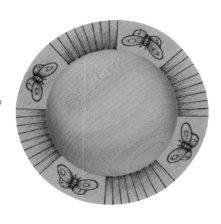

4 Add the finer detail to the inner part of the rim. Use an eraser to rub out any pencil lines visible after burning.

The finished bowl

The template used

Bread Board

This is a perfect example of an item that can be both useful and beautiful. The design of ears of wheat is ideal.

MATERIALS

- Plain wooden board
- Design to fit round the edge of the board
- Carbon paper
- Masking tape
- Ballpoint pen
- Drawing tip

TIP

To make it food safe, coat the board with pure sunflower oil, Tung oil or Danish oil.

The drawing used

The finished board

1 Fix the carbon paper and the design to the edge of the board with masking tape. Trace over the design firmly with the pen.

2 Make sure the design has transferred completely. Burn the outline of the design using the drawing tip.

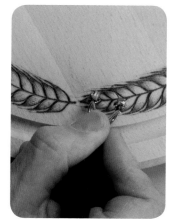

3 Shade in areas to add detail.

4 Finish shading the ears of wheat to complete the design.

Celtic Box

Celtic designs are always popular, but the intricacy of the pattern means it will take time to burn it, so you should support your wrist.

1 Layer the design and carbon on the lid of the box and fix down with masking tape.

2 Using the towel for support, trace over the design firmly using a ballpoint pen.

3 Peel back the carbon, making sure the design has transferred.

4 Burn the design using the drawing tip.

The finished box

5 Complete the shading on the box lid using the spoon point.

MATERIALS

- Small wooden box
- Design to fit the size of your box
- Carbon paper
- Masking tape
- Rolled towel
- Ballpoint pen
- Drawing tip
- Spoon point

TIP

Enlarge or reduce the image on a photocopier to fit the size of your box, then transfer using carbon paper.

The template used

Candlestick

The shape of the candlestick base meant that it was easier to draw the design freehand, using a sketch as inspiration, rather than a template.

MATERIALS

- Plain wooden candlestick
- Sharp pencil
- Drawing tip
- Eraser

TIP

Make sure you never leave an unattended candle burning.

The drawing used

1 Draw the design on to the base of the candlestick using a sharp pencil.

2 Burn the 'flame' shapes using the drawing tip.

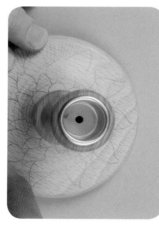

3 Add the detail. Use an eraser to rub out any pencil lines visible after burning.

Detail of the finished candlestick

Door Plaque

Children love to label their rooms, and this simply worked plaque has a space left for a name.

MATERIALS
- Wooden blank
- Templates
- Pencil
- Drawing tip
- Felt-tipped pens

TIP
Use artists' fixative or hairspray to fix the pen colours before varnishing or sealing.

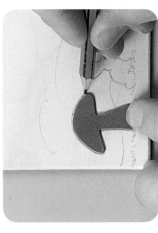

1 Draw the design in pencil, using the templates as appropriate.

2 Burn the outlines of the design using the drawing tip.

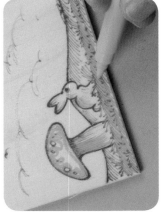

3 Start to add the shading.

4 Continue to add shading to complete the design.

5 Colour in the design if desired.

6 Add the finishing touches of colour.

The templates used

The finished plaque

Needle Case

This neat little container helps to keep needles safely in one place, and should delight any sewing enthusiast you know.

TIP

If you want to colour your design, water-based felt-tipped pens blend well and the texture of the wood will still show through.

The drawing used

1 Draw the design in pencil on the needle case.

2 Burn the outline of the design using the drawing tip.

3 Add the detail. Use an eraser to rub out any pencil lines visible after burning.

4 Add the dots beneath the solid lines.

5 Add colour as required.

The finished needle case

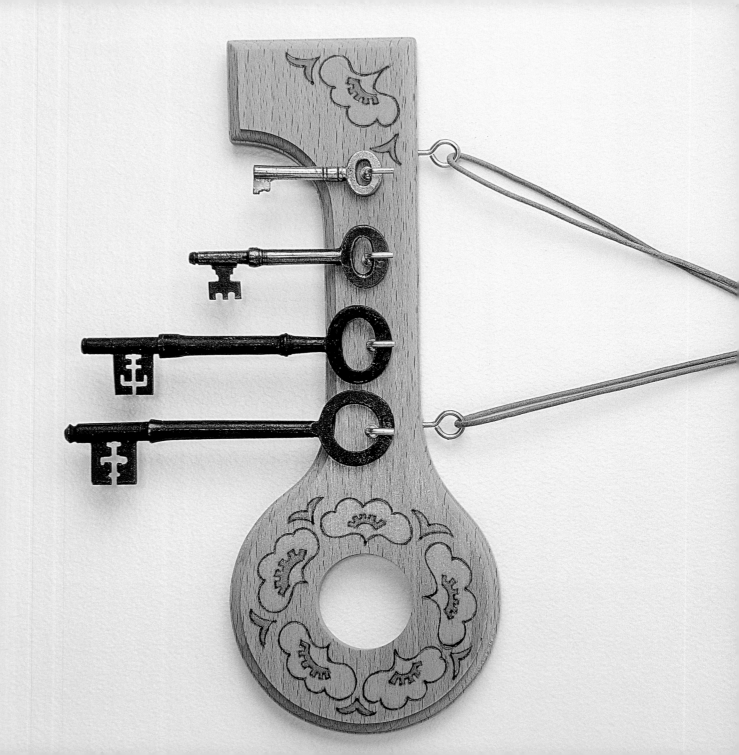

Key Rack

Every home has lots of different keys to look after, and this handy rack is an attractive way to keep them organized.

MATERIALS

- Wooden blank
- Design to fit the front of the blank
- Carbon paper
- Masking tape
- Ballpoint pen
- Drawing tip
- Acrylic paint
- Brush
- Varnish

TIP

With a name and date added, this would make an ideal 18th or 21st birthday present.

2 Trace over the design firmly using a ballpoint pen.

4 Burn the outline of the design.

1 Layer the carbon paper and the design and fix to the blank using masking tape.

3 Peel the carbon back carefully, making sure all the design has transferred.

6 Add colour, if desired, using acrylic paint. When it is dry, seal with varnish.

5 Complete the outline of the design.

The drawing used

Detail of completed design

Greetings Card

Burning a design on a piece of veneer makes an attractive panel for the front of a greetings card.

MATERIALS
- Small piece of veneer
- Pencil
- Drawing tip
- Eraser
- Felt-tipped pens
- Card stock
- Adhesive stick or glue

TIP
Burr maple, masur birch and bird's eye maple have interesting grain features that would work well as a background for the main design. Coloured veneers are also good for this project.

The drawing used

The completed design

1 Draw the design on the veneer.

2 Start to burn the outline of the design using the drawing tip.

3 Complete the outline. Rub out any pencil lines visible after burning.

4 Colour in and mount on the card using an adhesive stick or glue.

Techniques
Basic tool kit

I have used most machines available, from soldering irons to a hot wire machine. This is more expensive but is the choice of most professional pyrographers. Most people have well-stocked tool boxes but you may need to buy a few of the items below.

Control unit

This plugs into the mains and has a pilot light. The variable heat control knob produces a precise temperature.

Pen

This plugs into the unit and uses different tips. The spoon-point supplied is good for shading and calligraphy, and I make my own drawing nibs (see page 40).

Ruler

Use a ruler to create straight edges and map out patterns.

Carbon paper or transfer paper

Use with a hard, sharp pencil or ballpoint pen to trace the outlines of your design.

Scissors

For cutting carbon/transfer paper, card and drawing paper.

Wire/suede brush or sandpaper

This is useful for cleaning the wire nib of the pyrography pen.

Eraser

Use this to remove any pencil lines visible after the burning process.

Screwdriver

For changing wire nibs.

Pliers & flat-nosed pliers

For cutting the wire and shaping the nib.

Wire

This can be cut to size and used to form replacement nibs.

Masking tape

Use this to fix down carbon paper and drawings when transferring to the wood.

Pencil

B, 2B and HB pencils are useful for drawing designs.

Towel

Use a folded towel to support your wrist so bulky pieces are easier to work on.

Dust mask

This is essential to protect against inhalation of smoke.

Craft knife or pencil sharpener

Your pencil must be sharp for good, clear drawings.

Sandpaper

Use this to produce a smooth surface and to sand off small mistakes.

COLOURING MATERIALS

You can choose from all sorts of colouring materials to enhance your pyrography designs, from crayons to watercolours to coloured ink, and add highlights with gold- or silver-tipped pens, too. Most of the projects in this booklet use water-based felt-tipped pens, which blend well and still display the texture of the wood beneath, but objects that will be handled frequently should be coloured with permanent markers.

Choosing blanks

Blanks for pyrography are widely available. For just one item, try local hardware stores or the kitchen departments in major stores or supermarkets. Blanks are also available in bulk from specialist suppliers, which brings the price per item down considerably. You may have a friend who turns wood, which is how I obtain bowls and items such as needle cases.

Choosing different types of wood

From a distance, a pyrography design looks like a pencil drawing; close up, it resembles an engraving. Line quality varies, depending on the surface. On soft woods like pine, it tends to blur and run to create smoky areas. A line burnt on harder wood, such as sycamore, is cleaner and more exact. The woods used in this book are sycamore, beech and good-quality birch ply. Lime, holly and maple are also a good choice for pyrography, but soft woods tend to give an uneven line when burnt, and other types of wood may be too hard or too dark to produce a good effect.

Using templates

A wide variety of metal templates is available from specialist craft shops, and over the years I have built up quite a collection. Individual templates are reasonably priced, and they can be used again and again so they are good value. You could punch out your own card shapes, or cut designs from thin card using a pair of scissors as well as using plastic stencils.

Rubber stamps

When selecting rubber stamps, choose ones with clearly defined raised outlines and no blocked-in areas. The easiest ones to use are those made from clear plastic so that you can position them exactly as required on your chosen surface.

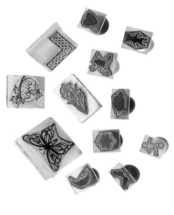

Making nibs

Nibs are shaped from nickel chromium wire. There are four grades: 26 SWG (finest), 25 SWG, 24 SWG and 23 SWG (thickest). The best one to use is 25 SWG. For most work, the wire is pinched to a point. Experiment to produce a range of shapes.

SPOON POINTS

Ready-made spoon points are available. They can also be made by twisting the U-shape to make a small circle at the tip. Hammer this out on a hard metal surface.

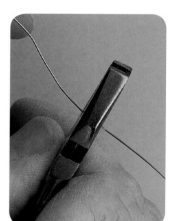
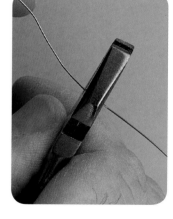

1 Cut a piece of 25 SWG wire, about 1¼in (3cm) long.

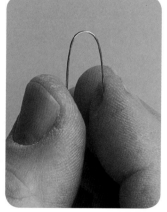

2 Hold the wire between your thumb and forefinger.

3 Bend into a U-shape.

4 Loosen the screws so the ends of the wire slide between the prongs and retaining grommets, then re-tighten.

5 Using pliers, pinch the loop to form a point.

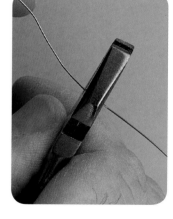

6 The finished nib.

Making marks

The art of successful burning requires concentration. The grain of the wood will either assist smooth flow or go against the direction of the tool. By varying the stroke, pressure and heat, it is possible to produce thin and thick lines, deep grooves, dots, textures and tones.

Hold the pyrography pen as you would a pen or pencil, and keep your fingers as near the nib as possible at the bottom of the black plastic sleeve. Do not touch the wire support as it can get very hot. For most woods, the heat control knob should be set so that the wire nib shows just a hint of red. Some woods require a higher heat setting, while veneer and materials like leather, card and hand-made paper need less heat. Too high a setting will cause scorching on either side of your burnt line.

The burning technique is similar to painting or sketching. Try to work with a smooth movement, starting at the top of the design and using light, short strokes. Work slowly, to give the wood time to burn. At first, you may get blobs and uneven lines, so it is important to keep practising.

Drawing tip

Spoon point

MAKING A SAMPLE BOARD

Take a small rectangle of birch plywood. Using a pencil, draw a random line (see below) or draw in a grid pattern. Burn the outlines and fill in sections using different techniques.

1 Pencil in a random outline.

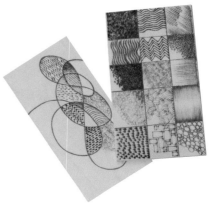

2 Burn the outline using a drawing point.

3 Fill in sections to practise and achieve different effects.

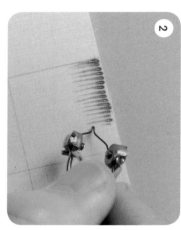

1 Work dots by stippling, just touching the tip to the wood.

2 Work short, straight lines, letting the wire rest for a bit longer at the beginning.

3 Work wavy lines, keeping the pressure on the tip as even as possible.

4 Cross-hatch small sections randomly to produce an interesting effect.

5 Shade diagonally, working a series of fine lines with even pressure on the nib.

6 Work dense stippling by burning tiny round shapes very closely together.

7 Work freehand circles for a decorative bubble effect.

WORKING EFFECTS WITH A SPOON POINT

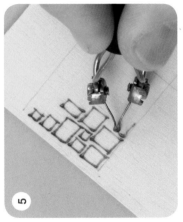

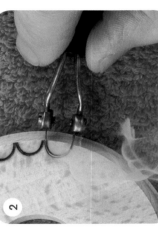

1 Work larger dots, letting the bowl of the spoon point rest on the surface.

2 Work diagonal shading as a series of fine lines.

3 Work spiral shapes with the inverted spoon point.

4 Work diagonal lines slowly to achieve a good burn.

5 Create a random brick effect with different-sized freehand rectangles.

DECORATIVE EDGES

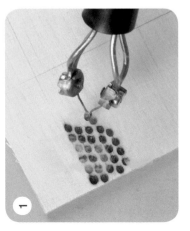

1 Using a U-shaped nib, on a flat edge.

2 Using a U-shaped nib, on a curved edge.

Lettering

Good lettering comes with practice. When you try forming these letters, remember to burn them in the direction shown by the arrows. The spoon tip is a good choice for lettering.

Draw the letters in pencil on ruled lines. Draft your letters on greaseproof or tracing paper first, to make sure they fit your chosen object. Use masking tape to stick the paper down if necessary. You can then use the paper as a template to work from.

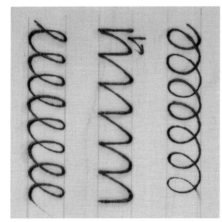

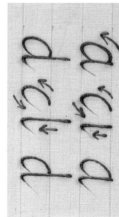

Try working the sample patterns (above) to train your hand and eye to produce shapes smoothly.

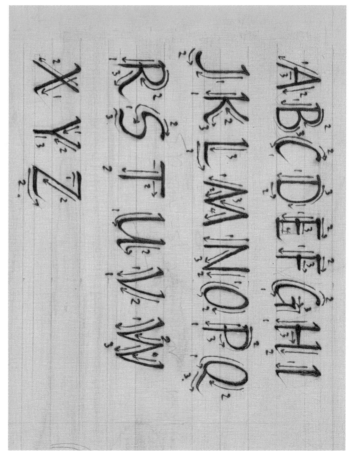

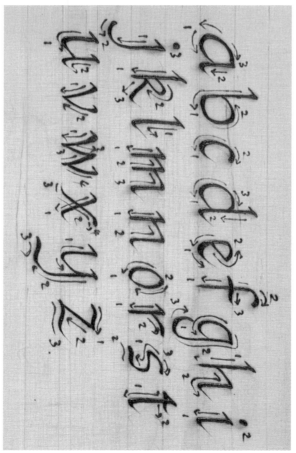

Follow the direction of the arrows on the sample letters (above and right) to work them.

Adding colour

In order to preserve the outline of the pyrography, it is best to use water-soluble paints such as acrylics or gouache. These can be diluted with water without losing colour strength. Water-based felt-tipped pens blend well and when paler colours are used, the various textures of the surface beneath show through the diluted colours. Use artists' fixative or hairspray to fix the pen colours before varnishing or sealing.

Water-based crayon

Felt-tipped pen

Permanent felt-tipped pen

Acrylic paint

Using water-based felt-tipped pens to build up layers of colour

Sketch books

Many artists carry a sketch book with them at all times and ideas can later be developed from any quick sketches. Ideas can come from observing man-made or natural objects. Look for interesting shapes, textures, colour or patterns. A sketchbook is like a visual diary; it is a resource that you can keep adding to and is always a source of inspiration.

Finishing your work

If left bare, the finished piece can pick up marks and get dirty. For pieces that are to be displayed outdoors, such as house numbers or house name plaques, you need to protect them with yacht varnish. A clear matt or satin varnish can be used for boxes that will be handled regularly. Beeswax is frequently used on finished items, or Danish oil, which can be brushed or wiped on and successfully brings out the grain of the wood.

Waxing using a soft cloth

Spraying with acrylic gloss varnish

Sanding off any rough edges

Safety information

Pyrography pen

- Do not touch any part of the hot wire nib with your fingers.

- Hold the pyrography tool as close to the nib as possible, but take care not to touch the metal elements. After long periods of working, the elements can become uncomfortably hot. Some models have guards to protect your hands.

- Keep the nib well away from your eyes.

- Make sure children are supervised when using pyrography equipment.

Ventilation

Make sure the room is well ventilated when you are working. Some surfaces, such as old wood, driftwood or leather, can give off nasty fumes. If you have an electric air purifier or a humidifier, use it to remove smoke from the work area.

Working with fixatives and sealers

- Take care that you do not breathe in fumes when you are working with fixatives, spray sealers or varnishes.

- Make sure the room you are working in is well ventilated (see left).

- Wear a dust mask to help prevent you breathing in fumes (see right).

- Always read carefully and follow the instructions given by the manufacturer regarding the use and storage of such products.

- Mop up any spills immediately using kitchen paper or rags, and dispose of them carefully.

- Take care to replace the lids of products securely after use.

Dust mask

A dust mask should always be worn when working. This will help to protect against breathing in smoke from the burning wood, or any dust particles produced when you are sanding your work.